Cumbrian Recipes

A selection of recipes from around Cumbria

By **Amanda Wragg**

BRADWELL
BOOKS

Published by Bradwell Books

9 Orgreave Close Sheffield S13 9NP

Email: books@bradwellbooks.co.uk

©Amanda Wragg 2013

British Library Cataloguing in Publication Data: a catalogue record for this book is available from the British Library.

1st Edition

ISBN: 9781902674865

Print: Cambrian Printers Aberystwyth SY23 3TN

Design by: Andrew Caffrey

Edited by: Louise Maskill

Photographic Credits:
  Joan Ransley & Shutterstock

Front Cover:
  Left to right: Joerg Beuge/Shutterstock; MShev/Shutterstock; violeta pasat/Shutterstock; alexpro9500/Shutterstock

Back Cover:
  Simon Baylis/Shutterstock

Title Page:
  Simon Baylis/Shutterstock

The photographs used in this book are to illustrate the dish and are not meant as a final representation of the finished result. Any garnish or additions are at your discretion.

Contents

Introduction

Cumbria is a relatively new county, established in 1974 and consisting of the ancient county of Cumberland along with parts of Lancashire and Westmorland, which no longer exists. It famously contains the Lake District, the largest National Park in the country and an Area of Outstanding Natural Beauty.

It's a landscape that sets spirits soaring and has been the inspiration for poets, painters and writers, not to mention climbers and walkers. Beatrix Potter, John Ruskin, William Wordsworth and Arthur Ransome made it their home and drew endless stimulation from the stunning countryside. It's been a draw for tourists for hundreds of years too, and these days there's another very good reason to visit.

Towering mountains, lush arable land and a stunning coastline are the backdrop for some of Britain's best food, with growers and makers providing top quality produce, from Ulverston in the south to Carlisle in the north. For years Cumbria's had a reputation for good hotels, restaurants and great pubs and now we can add artisan food producers to the impressive list.

Much of Cumbrian cuisine is based on dishes suitable for a hard working community living in a bracing climate. Cheap, simple and tasty meals were designed to feed hearty appetites and keep working families nourished.

More sophisticated produce is available these days, and in towns and villages you'll find great butchers, cheese and bread makers, fishmongers and impressive food stalls in street markets up and down the county. Local breweries are flourishing and small producers are finding national recognition; Kendal-based Demels chutneys, Holker Hall salt marsh lamb, Sarah Nelson's Grasmere Gingerbread and Cartmel sticky toffee pudding can be found in shops all over the country.

So head for beautiful Cumbria safe in the knowledge that you won't just encounter magnificent vistas, but that you'll find fabulous food whether you're eating in or out.

Simon Baylis/Shutterstock

Soda Bread

Baking is back! Making your own bread is very satisfying – and easy. This simple, straightforward recipe will become part of your weekly routine – you've got a home baked loaf in under an hour. Buttermilk is easy to buy in supermarkets these days – but if you can't get hold of it, use plain live yoghurt instead. Once you've made one you'll never go back to shop bought. **The smell in the kitchen whilst this is baking will send you off the scale!**

Ingredients

400g wholemeal flour

75g plain white bread flour

1 tsp sea salt

1 tsp bicarbonate of soda

425ml buttermilk or plain live yoghurt

Method

1   Preheat the oven to 390F/200C/gas 6. Put all the dry ingredients into a large bowl and mix together. Make a well in the centre and pour in the buttermilk or yoghurt. Using your hands mix all the ingredients until you've got a soft, slightly sticky dough.

2   Tip it out on to a lightly floured work surface and knead lightly for about a minute, just long enough to pull it together into a loose ball but no longer - you need to get it into the oven while the bicarb is still working.

3   Put the dough on a lightly floured baking sheet and dust generously with flour. Mark a deep cross in it with a sharp knife, cutting about two-thirds of the way through the loaf. Bake for 40-45 minutes, until the loaf sounds hollow when tapped underneath.

4   Cool on a wire rack if you like a crunchy crust, or wrap in a clean tea towel if you prefer a soft crust. Soda bread is best eaten while still warm, spread with salty butter and/or a dollop of your favourite jam or lemon curd. It makes great toast the next day – that's if you've got any left!

Space Monkey Pics/ShutterStock

Pickled Red Cabb

This tasty (and easy to make) accompaniment to cheese, meat and game is also a great idea for a present if you find a pretty jar to put it in. It takes a bit of time but it's worth it. It works brilliantly well with hotpot — in fact any stew or casserole. In our house we eat it by the barrel load, mainly with pork pies and cold ham. Apparently it was a favourite of Mrs Beeton. If it's good enough for her…

The cabbage is steeped in salt for about 3 hours then boiled for around 40 minutes.

Ingredients

500g red cabbage

140g sea salt

500ml cider vinegar

200ml red wine

400g granulated sugar

2 tsp black peppercorns

6 bay leaves

2 tbsp yellow mustard seeds

2 red chillies sliced very thin

age

Method

1. Place the shredded cabbage in a colander over the sink and sprinkle with salt. Leave for 2-3 hours, then drain and wash away the salt. Pay dry with a clean tea towel.

2. Put the vinegar, wine, sugar, peppercorns and bay leaves into a big, wide saucepan and simmer until the liquid has reduced by about half – about 40 minutes.

3. Strain through a fine sieve into a jug or bowl, and throw away the peppercorns and bay leaves. Put the cabbage, mustard seeds and sliced chillis into a big bowl then pour the strained liquid over.

4. Transfer the cabbage and pickling liquid into sterilized jars and screw the lid on tightly. It will last months in the fridge.

M. Unal Ozmen/ShutterStock

Cumberland Sauc

The precise history of this savoury sauce is a bit vague; one thought is that it originated in the late 19th century in Hanover and named after the Duke of Cumberland. What we do know is that it's delicious, and great served cold with pate, sliced ham or warm with sausage, gammon or game.

Ingredients SERVES 6

1 tbsp redcurrant jelly

500ml fresh orange juice

Zest and juice of ½ lemon and ½ orange

½ tsp mixed spice

1 measure of port

Method

1 Put all the ingredients in a pan. Reduce slowly until the mixture is halved.
   Top Tip: Keep an eye on it – it can boil over in an instant!

Ryzhkov Alexandr/Shutterstock

Simple Pasta Sauc

You know that feeling after a hard day's work, and you just want to throw a simple supper together? This delicious, easy tomato-based sauce is great with pasta – all you need add is a grating of parmesan, a sprinkling of basil and a glass of red wine. Sorted.

Ingredients SERVES 2

Olive oil

1 red onion, finely chopped

1 clove of garlic, finely chopped

A handful of black olives, stoned and halved

Pinch of chilli flakes

Tin of chopped tomatoes

1 tsp sugar

Sea salt

Freshly ground black pepper

4 basil leaves

Pasta of your choice – literally any will do; spaghetti, penne, linguine or those cute little bow ties

Freshly grated parmesan

Method

1. Warm a slug of olive oil in a frying pan. Add the chopped onion and garlic and cook gently until starting to colour. Add the chilli flakes, sugar, olives and the tin of tomatoes. Season to taste.

2. Let it bubble for about 15 minutes (adding a bit of water if it's starting to look dry)

3. In the meantime cook your pasta in a large pan of boiling salted water. Drain, put in warm bowls and drop the tomato sauce on the top. Add freshly grated parmesan and finish with torn basil leaves.

Joan Ransley

The Best Gravy ir

There are as many recipes for gravy as there are cookery books, but after a lifetime of trying to get it right, this is the fool-proof way to produce a golden brown, beautifully thick accompaniment to your Sunday roast.

Ingredients

Juices from the Sunday roast

1 tbsp plain flour

A splash of balsamic vinegar

2-3 dashes Worcestershire Sauce

Salt and freshly ground black pepper

ChameleonsEye/ShutterStock

Method

1   Scrape the bottom of the pan from your roast whilst the meat's resting and gather together all the sticky, brown, gooey bits in one corner of the pan. Mix the flour in and put the tin over two rings of the hob. Slowly, add a couple of tablespoons of boiling water and keep stirring as it thickens – keep adding water until it's lovely and thick.

2   Add the vinegar, relish and seasoning. Add another 300ml hot water and bring to the boil. Let it simmer for about 20 minutes – it will reduce a bit, leaving you with an intense, meaty, dark golden gravy that you can use with any number of dishes.

Christopher Elwell/ShutterStock

Vegetable Stock

Since time immemorial country people the world over have kept the stockpot simmering all day on the kitchen stove. Those days are pretty much gone, but making a good basic stock isn't difficult and although there are many quick options these days (even one or two of our 'top' chefs are advertising stock cubes!) there's nothing as satisfying as knowing your soup, stew or casserole is made with the real deal. This flavoursome stock will last for up to a week in the fridge, or batch freeze it for later use. Many cooks make different stocks depending on what they're the basis of; beef, fish, chicken – but I find this basic stock will do nicely for any dish you're making.

Ingredients

3 medium onions

5 medium carrots

3 medium leeks

3 sticks celery

8 cabbage leaves

Handful flat leaf parsley

3 sprigs fresh thyme

1 bay leaf

Sea salt

3.5 litres cold water

Method

1   Roughly chop the vegetables and put in a large saucepan or stockpot with all the other ingredients.

2   Cover with water and bring slowly to the boil.

3   Reduce the heat to a gentle simmer. Skim off any scum.

4   Simmer very gently with the lid ajar for an hour, skimming from time to time.

5   Strain through a sieve – don't push any of the soft vegetables through as the stock will become cloudy. Allow to cool then refrigerate.

Ben Smith/ShutterStock

Short Crust Pastry

Ready made pastry is a quick, convenient option if you're short of time, but if you'd rather make your own (it's simple enough) here's a fool-proof recipe that takes minutes to make, and just think of the brownie points you'll earn when the family knows you've made it from scratch!

Ingredients

125g plain flour

Pinch of salt

55g butter, cubed

40ml cold water

Method

1 Put the flour and salt in a large bowl and add the cubes of butter. Use your fingertips to rub the butter into the flour until you have a mixture that resembles coarse breadcrumbs – make sure you've no big lumps of butter left. Try to work quickly so that it doesn't become greasy.

2 Using a knife, stir in just enough of the cold water to bind the dough together. Wrap the dough in clingfilm and chill for 10 minutes before using. Once chilled, roll out on a lightly floured work top to the required size for your pie or pasty. Job done!

Valentina Proskurina/ShutterStock

Beetroot and Chee

This is a stunningly robust salad, full of earthiness and sweetness. Any soft cheese will do – goat's cheese works well. If you choose to cook the beetroot from scratch, allow an hour in the oven, but vacuum-packed cooked beets do the job just as well.

Ingredients SERVES 4

6 medium sized cooked beetroots (room temperature)

250g crumbly cheese

For the dressing

2 tbsp white wine vinegar

½ tsp Dijon mustard

5 tbsp olive oil

1 tsp caraway seeds

Sea salt and freshly ground black pepper

Slices of home made bread* to serve   * See page 6

Method

1   Mix together the vinegar, mustard and seasoning. Beat the olive oil in with a whisk, bit by bit. Toast the caraway seeds lightly under the grill then add them to the dressing.

2   Cut the beets into thick slices, add the dressing, crumble the cheese into chunks and scatter through the beets. Serve with thick slices of home made bread.

Melica/Shutterstock

noppharat/ShutterStock

Potted Char

A relative of the salmon, the char is found in the deep waters of the Lake District. Potted char has been considered a Cumbrian delicacy since the 16th Century and Charles Lamb mentions it in a letter to Samuel Taylor Coleridge in 1822. The fish has a delicate flavour and pink tinged flesh; this recipe is simple and rewarding – I often make it as a starter for a dinner party or it's great for a mid-week supper.

Ingredients SERVES 4

4 x 175g char fillets

7g ground mace

7g ground cloves

White pepper

50g butter

Method

1. Preheat the oven to 180C/350F/ gas 4. Place the char in a buttered ovenproof dish

2. Sprinkle with the spices and dot with butter. Cover with a lid or foil and bake for 30-35 minutes, basting occasionally.

3. Remove the fish and drain. Allow to cool then remove any skin or bones. Flake the fish, divide between 4 ramekins and press down firmly. Pour the melted butter on top then chill in the fridge.

4. Serve with a slice of lemon, brown buttered toast and a sprinkling of flat leaf parsley.

HLPhoto/Shutterstock

Butternut Squash &

This is a supremely warming, velvety winter soup, cheap and easy to make. Its dense, golden loveliness is enhanced with a swirl of cream on the top and if you're feeling flush, a scattering of croutons. The smell in the kitchen as this is cooking is worth the effort alone.

Ingredients SERVES 4

Splash of olive oil

1 large onion, finely chopped

1 butternut squash, peeled, de-seeded and chopped into chunks

1 red pepper, de-seeded and chopped into chunks

1 litre stock (see Basics or use Marigold Bouillon or Kallo cubes)

150ml skimmed milk

Sea salt

Freshly ground black pepper

Fresh chives or croutons, to garnish

Red Pepper Soup

Starters

Method

1   Warm the olive oil in a large pan and soften the onions. Add the squash, peppers and stock. Heat until simmering then cook gently for about 35 mins until the veg are tender.

2   Transfer to a blender and whizz until smooth. Return to the pan, add the milk and reheat. Season to taste.

3   Ladle into warm bowls. Swirl a dessert spoon of cream on the top of each one; add the chopped chives or croutons. This rewarding soup goes down well with a chunk of home made bread*

Joerg Beuge/Shutterstock

25

Smoked Trout or

There are several family firms smoking meat and fish in Cumbria; Bessy Beck Trout Fishery in Kirkby Stephen sells particularly sweet and fragrant smoked trout, and most supermarkets sell it. This dish is easy to throw together and incredibly versatile – it's great for a family supper but works just as well as a starter for a dinner party.

Ingredients SERVES 4

1 tbsp creamed horseradish

2 tsp white wine vinegar

1 small shallot, finely chopped

100g crème fraiche

Sea salt and ground black pepper

4 x 75g smoked trout (room temperature)

4 slices hot buttered toast

Lemon wedges

Toast

Method

1. Mix together the horseradish, chopped shallot, vinegar and crème fraiche. Season well - it benefits from a good grinding of black pepper and a proper pinch of salt.

2. Toast and butter the bread. Spread the horseradish mix on the toast, then top with the fish and a grind of black pepper over each one. Serve with a wedge of lemon.

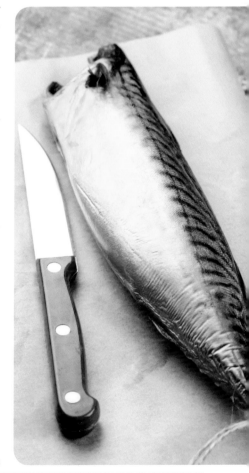

daffodilred/Shutterstock

Cumberland Tattie

Possibly the ultimate comfort food! There are as many versions of this classic Cumbrian recipe as there are lakes; this is the version my South Lakes mother in law makes. It's a gutsy, robust winter stew best served with mash and pickled red cabbage (see page 8).

Ingredients SERVES 6

2 tbsp plain flour

900g braising steak, cubed

225g lamb neck fillet, cubed

Vegetable oil

225g Black pudding

450g onions, roughly chopped

1 leek, washed and sliced

4 carrots, peeled and sliced

Half a swede, diced

450g potatoes, peeled and sliced ¼ inch thick

Beef stock (I use Marigold Bouillon or Kallo stock cubes)

Knob of butter

Sea salt

Freshly ground black pepper

Method

1 Preheat the oven to 160C/gas 3. Season the flour with salt & pepper. Toss the cubed lamb and beef in the flour.

2 Heat 2 tbsp of vegetable oil in a large frying pan. Fry the floured meat in batches to seal in the flavour. Transfer the meat to a casserole dish – one with a lid.

3 Fry the onions until they're transparent and add to the meat. Sweat the leek, carrots and swede in a little more oil and add those too. Cut the black pudding into chunks and add, stirring the whole thing thoroughly.

4 Add half the stock, cover and cook for about an hour; when the meat is tender, layer the sliced potatoes on the top, dot with butter, add the remaining stock, season and put back in the oven (having turned up the heat to 200C/gas 6) for about half an hour, til the potatoes are soft and golden.

Monkey Business Images/Shutterstock

Herdwick Lamb Co

This traditional, wholesome, rustic stew is made with Cumbrian lamb, a native breed living on the highest hills in central and western Lakes (and famously farmed by Beatrix Potter). The meat is well known for its distinctive flavour. Like most casseroles, this benefits from long cooking – and tastes even better the next day.

Ingredients SERVES 4

1 onion, finely sliced

1 clove garlic, crushed

1 large leek, chopped and washed

1 small turnip, diced

2 tsp rosemary, chopped

1 tsp thyme, chopped

1 tsp oregano, chopped

Sea salt & freshly ground black pepper

900g diced shoulder of lamb

1 litre stock (Marigold Bouillon or Kallo stock cubes are best)

28g pearl barley

28g plain flour, seasoned with salt & pepper

Oil for frying

For the dumplings

75g self raising flour

40g Atora suet

Sea salt

Freshly ground black pepper

1 tbsp chopped parsley

1 tbsp water

Method

1   In a large saucepan, warm some vegetable oil and add all the vegetables.
    Cook gently until they're transparent then add the herbs.

2   In the meantime toss the diced lamb in the seasoned flour and fry briskly in
    batches in another pan, until it's browned. Add the vegetables to the meat,
    plus the pearl barley and mix thoroughly. Add the stock and seasoning.
    Stir well and cover.

3   Simmer for about 1½ hours, until the meat is tender.
    Serve with floury potatoes.

For the dumplings

1   Put the flour, suet and parsley in a bowl. Season with salt & pepper.
    Stir in enough cold water to make a soft dough.

2   Shape with floured hands into
    8 balls. Uncover the casserole,
    pop the dumpling balls on top
    and leave the lid off.

3   Cook for a further 20 minutes
    until the dumplings have risen.

Paul Brighton/ShutterStock

Seafood Chowde

This is a British take on a New England recipe. A satisfying, robust and nutritious fish soup, you can make it cheaply (leave out the prawns!) or push the boat out if you're feeling flush. Either way, it's absolutely delicious, easy to make – and very filling!

Ingredients

2 tbsp olive oil

2 rashers smoked bacon

1 clove garlic, finely chopped

1 red pepper, skin off* cut into fine strips

1 ltr stock (Marigold or a Kallo cube)

250g naturally smoked haddock

250g salmon

500g new potatoes

330g can of sweetcorn

Pinch of chilli flakes

A squeeze of tomato puree

Freshly ground black pepper

8 king prawns

Small carton single cream

Method

1 Gently heat the oil in a thick-bottomed casserole dish. Fry the bacon until it's starting to colour. Add the garlic, chilli flakes and red pepper followed by the stock, fish, sweet corn, potatoes and the tomato puree. Grind over some black pepper and simmer for about 20 minutes (or until the potatoes are cooked.)

2 Turn the heat right down and add the prawns and cream. Put the lid on the casserole and cook very gently for a further 10 minutes. Serve in big bowls with chunks of home made bread.

*to skin a pepper, cut it in half, take out the seeds and place under a hot grill until the skin chars. Then put into a plastic bag and leave for 10 minutes – the skin will come off in one fell swoop!

bitt24/ShutterStock

Sweet Potato Bake

This simple recipe is a tasty vegetarian option and makes good use of Cumberland Farmhouse cheese from the Thornby Moor Dairy in Carlisle, which is well worth a visit. Carolyn Fairbairn has been a specialist cheesemaker since 1979 and her range of cow, ewe and goat's cheese is delicious.

Ingredients

500g sweet potatoes

25g ground cinnamon

115g crumbled Cumberland Herb

115g grated Farmhouse Cheddar

4 sage leaves

2 eggs

60ml milk

1 dessert spoon caster sugar

Method

1   Preheat the oven to 375F/190C/gas 5. Peel and dice the potatoes into large chunks and put in a pan with enough water to cover them. Bring to the boil and simmer for about 10 minutes, making sure they don't overcook.

2   Drain and place in a well-buttered ovenproof dish. Sprinkle with cinnamon, the sage leaves and then the cheeses. Beat the eggs, add the milk then pour over the potatoes and cheese.

3   Sprinkle the top with sugar and bake for about 25 minutes or until the top is golden brown. Served with green vegetables – green beans, broccoli or spring greens will do nicely.

mama_mia/ShutterStock

Hong Vo/ShutterStock

Salmon with Leeks

This simple dish is a reliable mid-week supper, and the fresh colours a delight. Freshwater salmon is caught widely in Cumbria, and goes particularly well with leeks.

Ingredients SERVES 2

4 medium leeks

40g butter

350g broccoli

2 tbsp plain flour

250ml vegetable stock (I use Marigold Bouillon or Kallo cubes)

2 fresh salmon fillets

50ml double cream

4 or **5** sprigs of dill

Sea salt

Freshly ground black pepper

& Cream

Method

1 Slice the leeks into thick discs and wash the grit out of them in the sink. Pat dry with kitchen roll and put them in a saucepan with the butter. Cook for about 15 minutes, stirring occasionally.

2 Break the broccoli into florets, then steam for a minute or two until tender. Stir the flour into the cooked leeks then add the stock. Simmer gently for about ten minutes until it thickens, stirring all the time. Put the fish into the pan with the leeks, spooning over some of the sauce. Season carefully, and add the dill. Finally add the cream. Cook over a low heat for about 5 minutes or until the fish is cooked.

Martellostudio/Shutterstock

Tlorna/Shutterstock

Steak, Kidney and Casserole

A traditional, rib-sticking dish with the unusual inclusion of beetroot, which not only gives it colour but lends a deep earthy taste – in a good way!

Ingredients SERVES 4

900g chuck steak cut into cubes

225g lambs kidneys, chopped

2 medium onions, roughly chopped

2 tbsp plain flour

1 tsp dried mixed herbs

400g beetroot cut into cubes (use the vacuum packed variety, not in vinegar)

½ litre beef stock (I use Marigold Bouillon or Kallo stock cubes)

Vegetable oil

Sea salt

Freshly ground black pepper

Beetroot

Method

1   Heat the oil in a large frying pan, add the onions and cook until they're soft and transparent. Add the cubes of steak and kidney and cook, stirring all the time, until the meat is evenly brown. Add the flour and stir in well – this will thicken the gravy.

2   Add the cubed beetroot, herbs and seasoning and gradually the stock. Bring the whole lot to simmering point, cover and cook for about 1 ½ hours or until the meat is tender. Check the seasoning and add more stock if it gets dry.

3   Serve with crushed new potatoes dotted with butter.

Africa Studio/Shutterstock

Paul Cowan/Shutterstock

Apple and Damso

Tansy is an ancient herb traditionally added to puddings; these days this sweet omelette or pancake is known as a Tansy. Damsons grow wild in the glorious Lythe Valley, south of Windermere, and you can often pick them up on roadside stalls in August and September.

Ingredients

2 large cooking apples, peeled, cored and thinly sliced
....
225g damsons, halved and stoned
....
15g butter
....
40g caster sugar
....
Pinch ground cloves
....
Pinch ground cinnamon
....
4 eggs, separated
....
3 tbsp creme fraiche or a couple of scoops of ice cream
....

Method

1	Put the apples, damsons, butter and half the sugar in a large frying pan. Cook over a gentle heat until the fruit softens, stirring all the time. Stir in the cloves and cinnamon then remove from the heat.
2	Beat the egg yolks with the cream and stir into the fruit. Whisk the whites until stiff, then fold in.
3	Cook over a low heat until the whole thing has set. Sprinkle the top with the remaining sugar then brown under a hot grill. Serve at once, straight from the pan, with crème fraiche or ice cream.

Sarah Marchant/Shutterstock

Julia Zakharova/Shutterstock

Grasmere Gingerb

Sarah Nelson's tiny bakery in Grasmere has been making this extraordinary gingerbread for 150 years; the exact recipe is a closely guarded secret, but this version is as close as can be. They're great dunked in tea, or crumble them over a dish of ice cream.

Ingredients

400g shortbread

170g demerara sugar

3 level tsps ground ginger

40g mixed peel, chopped

40g crystallized ginger, chopped

70g plain flour

1 pinch baking powder

80g golden syrup

70g unsalted butter

Method

1   Preheat the oven to 170C/325F/gas 3. Put the shortbread, sugar and
    2 teaspoons of the ground ginger in a food processor and whiz until the
    mixture resembles crumbs. Remove 100g of the mix and keep this to
    one side. Add the remaining teaspoon of ground ginger, the mixed peel,
    crystallized ginger, flour and baking powder to the processor and pulse until
    well mixed.

2   Melt the syrup and butter in a saucepan big enough to hold all the
    ingredients. When melted, add the mixture from the food processor and stir
    with a wooden spoon until everything is thoroughly mixed. Tip into a greased
    baking tray (about 20-35cm) and spread out evenly. Press the mixture down
    into the tray, using a spatula. When the mix is en even layer, put the tray in
    the preheated oven for 10 minutes.

3   Take the tray out of the oven and sprinkle the hot gingerbread with the
    reserved crumbs, pressing them down really well with a spatula. Carefully cut
    into good-sized pieces with a sharp knife, and leave to cool in the tray before
    eating. If you can resist.

Alexandra Lande/Shutterstock

B and E Dudzinscy/Shutterstock

Westmorland Pepp

A traditional fruit cake with a quirky Cumbrian twist – the addition of pepper. Don't panic, it brings a pleasurable, spicy dimension. Like a number of fruit cakes, this goes beautifully with cheese – so serve cold with a slice of award-winning Kendal Creamy cheese from the Rostock Dairy, available throughout Cumbria.

Ingredients SERVES 8

75g raisins

75g currants

100g caster sugar

75g butter

150ml water

225g self raising flour

1 tsp ground ginger

Pinch ground cloves

1/2 tsp finely ground black pepper

4 tbsp milk

1 medium egg, beaten

Method

1   Preheat the oven to 180C/350F/gas 4. Grease a deep 18cm cake tin. Put the fruit, sugar, butter and water in a pan and bring to the boil.

2   Simmer for 10 minutes then leave to cool. Sieve the flour into a bowl and add the spices and pepper. Gently stir in the fruit mixture, milk and egg. Mix thoroughly but don't beat.

3   Turn the mixture into the tin and bake for about 50 minutes; test it with a skewer – if it's done it will come out clean. *top tip; if the cake's not cooked but the top is getting brown, make a foil lid and put it on the tin. Turn out and cool on a wire rack

MShev/Shutterstock

Lakeland Plum Bre

This tea time favourite is a riff on a basic bread & butter pudding;
serve with cream, ice cream or custard, preferably in front of a roaring
fire on a winter's night - your kids will love you for it!

Ingredients

170g soft brown sugar

170g unsalted butter

4 tbsp golden syrup

140g sliced bananas

170ml oz milk

170ml whipping cream

8-10 slices of fruit loaf

Dessertspoon demerara sugar

Sultanas to top off

Method

1	Preheat the oven to 175C/350F/gas 4. Grease an ovenproof dish with butter.
2	Heat the milk and cream together gently. In another pan, heat the butter, sugar and syrup until well mixed, then add the bananas. Remove from the heat.
3	In a baking dish, layer the bread, milk mixture and banana syrup until you've used it all up. Sprinkle the top with demerara sugar and add a few sultanas to finish.
4	Bake for 20-25 minutes, or until the top is bubbling and golden. Serve piping hot with cream, crème fraiche or ice cream.

Jamie Rogers/Shutterstock

Cumberland Rum

This is one of the oldest traditional Cumbrian desserts dating back to the East Indies trading routes; Whitehaven was the second biggest port in the country and brought ginger, dates, rum, molasses and spices to Britain. Enterprising sailors invented a sweet, sticky flan from these items – it's assumed that the word 'nicky' derives from the fact that ingredients were often 'nicked' from the ship. Top tip; soak the raisins overnight in rum for a deeper flavour.

Ingredients

Packet of ready made short crust pastry (or make your own - see page 18)

For the filling:

280ml pint water

450g dates, chopped

4 pieces of stem ginger, chopped

120ml ginger syrup

50g raisins

Dark rum

Light brown sugar

1 small egg, beaten

Method

1 Preheat the oven to 180C/350F/gas 4. Mix the water, dates, stem ginger, ginger syrup and raisins together and simmer gently for 10 minutes. Leave to cool.

2 Roll out the pastry to ¼ inch thickness. Line a large flan dish with it (save the trimmings to make a lattice top). Add the filling. Make a pastry lattice for the top and glaze it with beaten egg. Sprinkle with light brown sugar.

3 Put in the middle shelf of the oven for 20 minutes or until the pastry is golden brown.

4 Brush with rum whilst it's still warm, and serve with a dollop of crème fraiche.

Jamie Rogers/ShutterStock

Corned Beef Hash

An old family favourite, this hearty, easy to make comfort dish is a
good way of using left over vegetables. A fried or poached egg turns
this quick supper into a more substantial dinner.

Ingredients

400g swede, peeled and diced

700g potatoes, peeled and diced

300g carrots, peeled and diced

2 tbsp sunflower oil

1 red onion, peeled and thinly sliced

175g tin of corned beef

1 tbsp tomato puree

Dash of Worcestershire sauce

Freshly ground black pepper

Method

1   Bring a large pan of water to the boil and cook the diced swede for 5 minutes. Add the potatoes and carrots and cook for a further 10 minutes. Drain well.

2   Meanwhile, heat the oil in a large frying pan and add the onion. Cook over a medium heat until softened – be careful not to let them burn.

3   Roughly mash the drained vegetables so they still have some texture. Break the corned beef up and fold into the veg. Put it in the pan with the onions, add the tomato puree and Worcestershire sauce and mix well. Add a couple of twists of black pepper and continue cooking for a further 10 minutes, stirring gently until piping hot.

jabiru/Shutterstock

Macaroni Cheese

This recipe calls for one or two more ingredients than a regular macaroni cheese but it's a winner, the family will love you for it. Serve with a simple green salad dressed with a squeeze of lemon – the richness of the dish needs a sharp accompaniment.

Ingredients SERVES 4

175g dry macaroni

1-2 tbsp olive oil

4 slices of smoked bacon cut into small pieces

1 medium onion, finely chopped

75g chestnut mushrooms, sliced

1 x 150g ball mozzarella cheese

300g tub of cheese sauce (most supermarkets do one)

2 tbsp crumbled Cumberland Farmhouse

1 bunch vine tomatoes

Sea salt

Freshly ground black pepper

Method

1   Preheat the oven to 375F/190C 190C/gas 5. Fill a large saucepan with
    water and bring it to the boil. Add a teaspoon of salt and a splash of olive oil.
    Add the macaroni and cook it for 5 minutes.

2   Meanwhile, heat the oil in a frying pan. Add the onion and bacon and cook
    for a couple of minutes, until both are golden brown. Add the mushrooms
    and cook for a further 2 minutes. Cut the mozzarella into smallish cubes.

3   Drain the pasta and put it into an oven-proof dish. Add the contents of the
    frying pan, the cheese sauce, the diced mozzarella and a good grinding of
    black pepper. Sprinkle the cheese over the top. Stir everything through and
    place the tomatoes (still on the vine) on top.

4   Drizzle olive oil on the tomatoes. Place the dish on the high shelf in your oven and
    bake for 20 minutes, or until the cheese is bubbling. Serve piping hot with a salad.

Elena Shashkina/ShutterStock

Potted Shrimps

The good people of Cumbria have been enjoying this dish for centuries; it's versatile in that you can make it into a starter or snack. It has famously been made and sold in tubs by the Baxter family from Morecambe Bay since 1799 and the precise recipe is a state secret, but this is a good approximation. Pouring a layer of clarified butter on the top is an ancient way of preserving the food underneath.

Ingredients

200g unsalted butter

Juice of 1/2 lemon

¼ tsp ground mace

¼ tsp ground nutmeg

¼ tsp white pepper

½ tsp anchovy paste or Gentleman's Relish

200g cooked and peeled brown shrimps

Cayenne pepper

Method

1   Melt the butter in a pan over a gentle heat and allow to simmer until you
    spot the first dark flecks – watch it carefully, or it will burn. Strain through two
    sheets of kitchen roll, into a jug.

2   Wipe out the pan, and pour in two-thirds of the butter. Add the lemon juice,
    mace, nutmeg, pepper, anchovy essence and a pinch of salt and simmer
    very gently for five minutes, then take off the heat and allow to cool but not
    set. Divide the shrimps between 4 ramekins, pressing them in tightly.

3   When just warm, but still liquid, divide the spiced butter between the
    ramekins and put in the fridge to set. Once solid, pour over the remainder of
    the clarified butter and return to the fridge to set.

4   Serve with a sprinkle of cayenne pepper and hot toast.

Subbotina Anna/Shutterstock

Herdwick Burger

Everyone has their favourite way of making burgers; I've added beaten egg and breadcrumbs at different times in an effort to bind the ingredients but in the end I've opted for the simple approach, which seems to work nicely. The ginger and cumin are optional but give the burger a piquant kick. The jury is out on the beef/lamb debate but I always prefer to use minced lamb.

Ingredients

1 tbsp oil or butter

1 large onion, finely chopped

1kg roughly minced Herdwick lamb (or any non-lean mince)

Knob of fresh ginger, grated

1 tsp ground cumin

1 tsp chilli flakes

2 tsp chopped herbs (parsley or thyme work well)

1 tsp salt

Black pepper

Garnishes, sauces and rolls, as desired

Method

1   In a large bowl, mix all the ingredients together thoroughly with your hands.

2   Divide the meat into 12 balls (wet your hands to stop the meat from sticking). Cover and refrigerate for half an hour.

3   Remove from the fridge. Sprinkle a film of seasoned flour on your worktop and roll each ball in it, gently flattening the balls into flat shapes about an inch thick.

4   Cook the burgers on a medium to hot barbecue or griddle pan: leave them undisturbed for the first 3 minutes so they build up a good seal on the bottom then carefully turn them over. Keep a close eye on them if you're barbequing; if the flames are fierce they'll burn.

Expoz Photography/ShutterStock

Cumberland Sau
Bean Casserole

Probably the most famous dish from Cumbria is the Cumberland sausage, coiled up and often bought by length rather than weight. It's available all over the country, but for me, it tastes better bought and eaten in the county! Every local butcher sells it; this simple, one-pot recipe is a standby in our house, summer and winter! The harissa paste gives it a piquant kick.

Ingredients SERVES 4

A large coil of Cumberland sausage

Carton of tomato passata

1 tin of red kidney beans

1 tin of butter beans

1 tsp English mustard

1 tbsp wholegrain mustard

1 tbsp harissa paste

4 tomatoes

Flat leaf parsley to garnish

age and

Method

1	Preheat the oven to 230C/450F/gas 8. Grill the sausages under a medium heat for 10 minutes – don't let them brown, just cook through.
2	Put the beans, passata, harissa and mustard into a casserole dish (one that has a lid). Cut the partially cooked sausages into chunks and add them to the dish, stirring everything thoroughly. Cut the tomatoes in half and place on top. Cook for 30 minutes on the middle shelf of the oven.
3	Serve piping hot with mashed potatoes.

Apolonia/Shutterstock

Shepherd's Pie

Cottage pie (made with beef) or Shepherd's pie (made with lamb) are the kings of comfort food, can be made a day in advance (tastes even better) and represents great value for money! I like to sprinkle a handful of strong cheese on top: young cheesemaker Martin Gott makes a fabulous ewe's milk cheese, the multi-award winning St James which is deliciously smoky, and can be found in his fabulous shop in Cartmel.

Ingredients SERVES 4

Vegetable oil

100g lean lamb mince

1 large onion, finely chopped

1 carrot, finely chopped

2 celery sticks, finely chopped

Clove garlic, finely chopped

6 mushrooms, sliced

1 sprig thyme

200ml stock (Marigold is the best, but any good stock cube will do)

Worcestershire sauce

1 tin chopped tomatoes

450g potatoes

Knob of butter

Salt

Freshly ground black pepper

Handful of grated or crumbled cheese

Method

1   Heat a tablespoon of oil in a large pan and gently brown the mince. Remove and add the chopped vegetables to the pan. Cook for about five minutes or until they've softened a bit.

2   Add the mince, a good dash of relish, the tomatoes, stock, thyme and season generously with salt & pepper. Let it bubble away for about an hour, until the stock has reduced by half.

3   In the meantime, peel the potatoes, cut them into small-ish chunks, put in cold water with a pinch of salt and bring to the boil. Let them simmer away for about 20 minutes, until they're soft.

4   Drain, add a knob of butter, a splash of milk, and mash. Put the mince mixture into an ovenproof dish, cover with the mashed potatoes, sprinkled on the cheese and put in a medium hot oven for about 15 minutes until the cheese has browned up. Serve with minted peas and pickled red cabbage.

violeta pasat/Shutterstock

Salmon with Samp

This is a great dish for a special occasion and makes good use of samphire, a delicious, nutritious sea vegetable found on the coastline (and in most good supermarkets).

Ingredients

4 salmon fillets

Sea salt to season the fish

75g butter

115g samphire

Flat leaf parsley to garnish

For the crab accompaniment

115g white crab meat

2 tsp finely chopped capers

2 tbsp flat leaf parsley, chopped

1 tbsp chives, chopped

2 hard boiled eggs, finely chopped

3-4 tbsp extra virgin olive oil

1/2 lemon, juice only